IMAGES
of England

AROUND
HAMBROOK

'O Who will o'er the Downs so Free'
by Robert L. de Pearsall

O who will o'er the downs so free,
O who will with me ride,
O who will up and follow me
To win a blooming bride?
Her father he has locked the door,
Her mother keeps the key;
But neither door nor bolt shall part
My own true love from me!

I saw her bow'r at twilight gray,
'Twas guarded safe and sure,
I saw her bow'r at break of day,
'Twas guarded then no more!
The varlets they were all asleep,
And none was near to see
The greeting fair that passèd there
Between my love and me!

I promised her to come at night,
With comrades brave and true,
A gallant band with sword in hand
To break her prison through:
I promised her to come at night,
She's waiting now for me,
And ere the dawn of morning light
I'll set my true love free!

This glee is believed to have been written in the dining room at Sturden Court Farm, and is said to refer to the elopement of Hugo de Sturden with a lady from Syston (see p. 102). The author lived from 1795 to 1856.

IMAGES
of England

AROUND
HAMBROOK

Compiled by
Sydney Marks

TEMPUS

Tempus Publishing Limited
The Mill, Brimscombe Port,
Stroud, Gloucestershire, GL5 2QG

ISBN 0 7524 2205 7

Typesetting and origination by
Tempus Publishing Limited
Printed in Great Britain by
Midway Colour Print, Wiltshire

This book is dedicated to my wife, Audrey Marks

Whiteshill Council School, *c.* 1926. The 'clinic' building has yet to be built. The red-brick council houses of Worrells Lane (right) were started in 1920; the author lives in one of them.

Contents

Introduction

Hambrook lies about five miles north east of the centre of Bristol and is governed by Winterbourne Parish Council and South Gloucestershire Council. Hambrook does not have a parish of its own, with half of the area lying in Frenchay and the rest under the control of Winterbourne Down Proverbial Church Councils. The River Frome flows through the area and is joined by Bradley Brook and The Stream.

Hambrook has its first traceable mention in the *Domesday Book* in 1086. It states that Geoffrey, Bishop of Coutances in Normandy, held 'Hambroc' in the reign of William the Conqueror as a reward for having served with William during the invasion in 1066.

Early in its history the village was involved in the wool trade. A good water supply ensured power for a number of corn mills on the river and small quarries around the village provided a steady supply of the local red pennant stone, a good material for building. The village has long had many large houses which were erected by the richer citizens of Bristol, who recognized the village as an attractive area to live but convenient for the city. These large houses gave employment to local people as maids, cooks, gardeners etc.; some houses had a staff of up to ten people. Hambrook today is in a Conservation Area, so much of the village's rich history is now preserved. It is of particular interest from an architectural point of view, with small cottages and large houses mostly dating from the seventeenth and eighteenth centuries. Hambrook was also remarkable for a village of its size in having a hospital, founded in 1867 by Dr Edward Crossman.

The farming community has also seen many changes. Once, most of the farmers grew their own root crops of mangolds, swedes, turnips and kale, which besides being sold to shops would also feed the cattle, sheep and horses during the winter months. Wheat, barley and oats were also cultivated, while the grass was grown, cut and dried in stacks that we knew as haymows, which were thatched with straw to keep out the rain. This was one of the skilled jobs done by farm labourers, and their handiwork would often last for a couple of years. The harvest would be threshed out mostly by steam-driven machinery. Operating the threshers was a very dusty job, but also exciting as the mice and rats scuttled out of the stores where they had made a home for themselves. The long hours of farm labourers also included work with stock, maintenance of machinery, hedging and ditching.

Childhood Memories

These paragraphs are extracts from the memories of Leslie John Henry Harrison, the author's cousin, who was born in 1910 and died in 1984 They relate to several of the areas portrayed in this book.

I remember Gran and Gramp moving from Church Cottage to Brookside Cottage, Pye Corner. After all the things had gone off in the big hay cart, Gramp and I walked down Bradley and across the fields, under the railway tunnel which was for cattle and people, down the Barton, across the ford to the cottage. The ford was no longer in general use except for very heavy loads; a bridge had been built over the river to get to the Butchers' and to the lane leading up to the Barton and the road had been what they called 'metalled' or made of hard rolled stones, from where it left the road to where it joined the Barton lane. Amos's old house, which was below the ford lane, was now quite below the bridge road as well. At the junction of the two roads was the local general shop, Mrs Clay's, and on down the lane on the right was a cottage where the Maby family lived – they had come recently from South Wales. On the left further down was an offshoot into The Barton, which was like a small square with four cottages facing towards the lane, while one which was the continuation of Gramp's new cottage faced inwards towards them. Gramp's cottage faced the lane and the garden went right down to the water's edge, opposite to two ruined cottages whose gardens went right back to the bridge road but well below its surface.

Worthy and Jim and I used to go paddling down the brook, lifting stones ever so gently and stabbing eels with a fork, the prongs of which were held tightly between finger and thumb. Gramps also used to take me to the brook to look for wild watercress. Also down the brook was a place called the Lilacs where the water ran much deeper, and the flowers here in the spring were glorious. In the autumn there were hazel nuts to be gathered.

I remember going to Whiteshill School. This is where I had my first taste of growing things, as the school had a little garden alongside it. I also remember the First World War Armistice [11 a.m. on 11 November 1918], when a great big bonfire was built on some ground beside the school gardens. This huge bonfire was lit on the evening of the day the Armistice was signed, after everybody had had a good day of fun and games. I remember sack races, egg-and-spoon races and all sorts of things to eat that we weren't used to – oranges, bananas, jellies, sweets and chocolates. In the evening with the fire we had roast chestnuts, roast potatoes, ham rolls, lemonade and cider. I remember the fire was so big that it burnt for three days before the ashes cooled off.

Some of the children I went to school with then were Alan Maggs (Rusty, my greatest pal), Harry Edwards, his brother Joe and sister Annie, Ken Malpass and his brothers Dennis and Tony, Reg Mabey, Alan Guy, Frank Edwards, Bertie Adams and so on. I had a nickname through playing with Rusty and Frank among the conker trees on the Common – it was 'Hangman'. I think Uncle Worthy gave it to me because I had tied Rusty up in the tree and in trying to get loose he nearly hanged himself. We used to go scrumping in Dr Crossman's orchards, after apples, pears, plums and medlars, even though these things were to be had in plenty in our own gardens. This orchard was alongside the chapel, which, with much of the local population having come from Wales, was a typical one, preaching hell and damnation, and with a Welsh type of choral singing. Uncle Jim used to work at Dr Crossman's stables and garages – he had had practice with horses and the doctor kept two or three hunters to ride and show at local horse shows. He [Uncle Jim] could also drive a car and look after the engineering side of things. He was a general handyman as well and looked after the acetylene gas lighting system.

Acknowledgements

I would like to thank the following people for their help: Mr and Mrs D. Fitz, Mr W. Amos, Mrs P. Shaw, Mr J. Bartlett, Mr & Mrs J. Lewis, Mr A. Freake, Mr M. Tozer, Mrs N. Evans, Mr G. Crew, Mr M. Davis, Mr K. Harris, Mr P. Adams, Mr R. Collett, Mr R. Close, Mr H. Hathaway. I would also like to thank all the people who have lent me photographs whose names I have forgotten. Special thanks, too, to Letty Fitz for all the typing she has done for me.

About the Author

Sydney Thomas Marks was born at Pye Corner, Hambrook, in 1933. He went to the local school from the age of three to fifteen and attended Whiteshill Congregational church (now Whiteshill Evangelical church) for many years before transferring to All Saints' church, Winterbourne Down. He worked at Bristol Pottery, Fishponds, for twenty-one years until the factory closed. He left the village in 1956 after marriage but returned in 1979 to live with his mother. Every Sunday evening she had a visitor named Bert Fowler who looked upon Sydney as a son. He had unfortunately lost his own son at the age of twelve years; this young lad was the same age as Sydney. It was Bert who got him interested in local history. He passed on family photographs, diaries, knowledge of the village band, Whiteshill Congregational church and local schools. He would borrow photographs from his friends for Sydney copy.

Sydney was also a good racing cyclist, being the only rider to win the West of England Time Trial Championship and the Western Road Race Championship, a record that still stands today.

It has been a pleasure to record these notes and to help in typing the captions.

Letty Fitz

One
Shops and Inns

The hub of the village, including the bakery, post office and grocery store, dates back to around 1700. In 1831 Nathaniel Good was the baker; the business stayed in his family until 1932 when the Turners took over. It closed in 1997.

Mr Sydney Good and his three daughters are ready for a cycle ride. Mrs Good is in the doorway. Note the word 'Hambrook' engraved in the upstairs window sill.

Mrs Good outside her shop, *c.* 1922. The motorcycle, registered AE8436, is a Royal Ruby with a $2\frac{1}{2}$hp belt-driven engine.

The post office moved from beside the bakery into the next-door building. In later years the post office was taken over by the Carpenter family. In 1950 Mr and Mrs Shepherd took over until it closed in 1970.

The Winterbourne bus on its return journey to Bristol, stopping at Good's shop, *c.* 1914. The two cottages by the bus have since been taken down and replaced by a modern building called Crossman House.

A queue for bread in 1943, during the Second World War. This, however, was no ordinary ration queue; Mr Turner is handing out free bread generously donated by an American soldier who was stationed at nearby Frenchay Hospital.

Hambrook Post Office in the early twentieth century. The delivery cart at the junction is from the bakery.

E. Good, grocer, was a relative of Sydney Good the baker. These village children also appear in other photographs. The shop was also owned by Miss Clara Good, who sold corn and meal, which were in demand as most people kept poultry.

Another view of Good's shop. On the left of the shop is the owner's residence, called Myrtle Cottage. In the distance is the White Horse inn.

A busy street scene from the early years of the twentieth century. There is a delivery boy with his basket, a man pulling a very large hand cart, and a pony and trap waiting for its owner.

Over the years Good's grocery shop was enlarged. Mr Harrison took over in 1935 and continued as the shopkeeper until 1946.

The next owner of the shop was Mr George Bracey, from 1946 until 1960. The post office was added in the late 1940s. The bicycle belonged to Barbara Thornell who cycled from Stoke Gifford to work in the shop. The bell on the roof was rung for local workers in premises behind the shop at start and finish times.

The inauguration of Hambrook Women's Institute Jubilee Seat, commemorating the Silver Jubilee of Queen Elizabeth II, in 1977. From left to right, standing: Edna Hill (with child), Violet Elson, Sylvia Hart, Madge Hutton, Rose Brooks, Ethel Bracey, Helen Hughes, Monica Ashford, Susan Cuff (with child), Edna Holt. Seated: Fay Hutchinson, Pete Maggs, Brenda Kislingbury. When the shop closed the seat was moved to Whiteshill Common.

The Firs, or Sandy's the butchers. The shop is to the left, in the middle is the slaughterhouse and the residence is on the right. The slaughterhouse was formerly a malt house. In 1889 William Tanner leased it to Thomas Sandy and it was then bought by his son T.G. Sandy and passed on to M.F Sandy. Both the butcher's and the slaughterhouse closed in the 1980s.

Pullin's shop started life as a car repair garage in the first decade of the twentieth century. It burnt down in the mid-1920s and re-opened after repairs as a general stores. Austin Pullin passed it on to his son, Sid, who added a barber's section at the rear. The shop now incorporates the Post Office and is the only shop left in the village.

The Crown. Although the building is older, records only date back to 1827 when the owner was J. Evans. In 1889 it was purchased by Bristol United Breweries. On the forecourt was a weighbridge where loads could be weighed for 2d. The office can be seen on the left. On the right by the lady was Mr Coombes' shoe repairs shop.

A load of hay is being weighed on the Crown weighbridge while the pony has his feed on the village green.

The Crown Inn in around 1912, when the horse and cart still ruled the road. The cart here belongs to a travelling hardware salesman, R.E. Coates of Easton Road, Bristol. Village children have also gathered and the man right of centre is Mr Coombes, the cobbler.

An enlargement of the group of children in the previous photograph. Harold Pendock is the boy in the blazer and the lad with the bicycle is Harry Amos.

A delivery of beer to the Crown by Bristol United Brewery. On the cart is Harry Amos, while Mr Kiff the dray man is holding the horse. In the doorway is Fred Amos, the father of Harry and Fred, and the landlord Albert Amos is sitting on the barrels.

Sitting on barrels outside the Crown, before 1916. From left to right: Sid Mapstone, John Carpenter, Harry Amos, Albert Amos (landlord). In the window is Emily Organ, sister of Maurice Organ who became the next landlord in 1916. When he died in the 1950s his daughter, Betty, took over.

The White Horse inn, 1930s. Three forms of transport are evident in this view – bicycle, motorcycle and motor car. Jeremiah Emery was the landlord from the 1920s until the 1940s, and then his daughter took over with her husband, Bill Hutton.

The Malthouse of the White Horse inn. In 1810 William Gayner of Filton had 45 bushels of barley made into malt here, at William Bowen's at Hambrook. In later years the building was used as a changing room for Hambrook Football Club.

The Black Horse inn. This hostelry has seen many changes in its name over time; it has been known as the Steak House, the Hambrook inn, and is now simply the Hambrook. Landlords have been Edward Luton, William Luton, Mrs Mary Mapstone, Henry and May Anstey. Mr Anstey also ran the adjoining market gardens. The Ansteys ran the pub for thirty-seven years.

In this Edwardian view, the lady is standing by the bridge over the river known as Bradley Brook at the rear of the White Horse inn. Note the well-kept garden of the inn.

The White Horse and Black Horse inns, not long after 1911. At the centre of the junction is oak tree planted to commemorate George V's Coronation in 1911. There is a high-quality carriage outside the White Horse. The Malthouse is the white building along the roadside behind the pub. At this point the Black Horse was selling Thomas's home-brewed beer. In the distance is Rock House.

Two
People and Places

Formerly known as Griffin's Tenement, Hambrook House was one of the properties held by the Bayly family in the 1600s. The house was enlarged in 1714 and the Georgian façade was added in 1794.

In the orchard of Hambrook House is this spire. It was taken down from Winterbourne church when it was struck by lightning in 1827 and rebuilt as a folly with the ice house underneath by Revd John Pring, the then owner. Revd Pring was the headmaster of Winterbourne Church of England School.

Over the doorway to the ice house, beneath the spire, stands the word 'Gerizim', the Hebrew name of one of a pair of Old Testament mountains. Its twin, 'Ebal', may be around somewhere else in the grounds! 'Gerizim' is translated as 'Mount of Blessing' in the Book of Joshua, chapter 8, verse 33. In the ice-house doorway a plaque has been erected which reads: 'This listed building was restored and the weather vane erected to celebrate the 60th wedding anniversary of Richard & Mary Carlton on the 20th April 1995. This plaque is dedicated to the memory of Mary Carlton MBE who died July 27th 1995.'

Hambrook Grange dates back to the seventeenth century; coins from the Stuart period have been found here. There is an oak staircase made from solid blocks of wood.

The old corn barn at Hambrook Grange. The building has recently been restored and tastefully converted into two dwellings.

The Stream, Hambrook, with old cottages leading to Fabers Farm, middle right.

Faber's Farm is the oldest known house in the village. In 1634 it was described as Faber's Place and in 1638 Thomas Bayly purchased it. He owned many other houses in the neighbourhood. It remained in the Bayly family until 1796.

THE MILL, HAMBROOK, NEAR BRISTOL.

The stream at Faber's Farm, with some workers taking a break on the bridge in the 1930s. The caption on the postcard relating to 'the Mill' is misleading as no records exist of a mill on this site.

The stream once again alongside Faber's Farm; it runs in the ditch behind the railing.

Hambrook Court. The original house on this site was the Manor Court of Hambrook. One tenant in 1826 was Lt-Col. Thomas Bereton, who was in charge of troops during the Bristol Riots in 1831. He was brought before a court martial to answer for his handling of the unrest and committed suicide on the fourth day of his trial.

Hambrook Court became a home and surgery for the village doctors from around 1870 until the 1950s. Dr Eadon ran the practice from 1897 to the 1920s. He is seen here on his rounds with his Quadrant motor cycle in 1905/06.

Hambrook Grove, originally known as the Green Estate. In 1700 Thomas Grant conveyed it to Joseph Bayly who also owned Faber's Place.

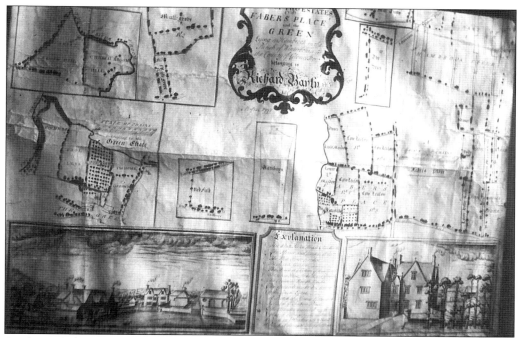

A plan of the estates made before 1778, showing 'Faber's Place' to the right of centre. Hambrook Grove is on the left, and there are also plans of the fields.

This drawing was made at the same time as the plan on the previous page. On the left is the White Horse inn, referred to by Henry Fielding in his *History of Tom Jones* written in 1749. In the centre is Hambrook Grove and on the right are the stables. Note the distinctive round windows and doorways.

The stables at Hambrook Grove today. The round window is still there and the original shape of the doorways can still be discerned in the stonework, although today's doors are smaller.

Hambrook Grove passed into the hands of the Mirehouse family from 1832 until the 1960s. For much of this period, many servants were employed, one of whom was Laura Cook, the author's aunt, seen here around 1925. In 1851 there were seven servants who lived in.

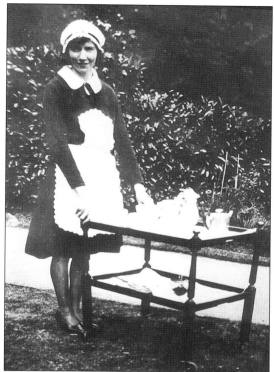

This well stands in the grounds in front of Hambrook Grove house.

The Green and Grove View, the four Georgian cottages which in 1827 were all owned by Samuel Clarke. This photograph probably dates from the 1920s or 1930s.

The Green once again. The house on the right is Evancoyd, formerly called Waylands. From 1837 it was the home of doctors – first Dr Thomas Day, then his son, Dr Edwin Day. The cottage on the left is called Chestnuts.

Grove View is on the left and the entrance to Hambrook Court is on the right. The long skirt of the lady on the left and the costumes of the two girls date this picture to the Edwardian period.

The main road through the village, early twentieth century. Good's shop is on the right. The footpath in the foreground is now gone, having been lost to road widening. On the right, note the distinctive arch gateway. There are several others of the same style around the village.

This is the house behind the arch gateway shown on the previous page. It is unusual for this district in that it has three storeys. In 1956 it was sold for £1,350.

The same house in winter.

The house nearer to the camera, St Dunstan, home of Mrs Clutton who was a school teacher, was pulled down for the building of the M4 motorway which went right through the village in the late 1960s. At the rear of the house the workshop can be seen where Mr Pendock, the undertaker, made his coffins.

Village children who lived in the cottages pose for the camera, c. 1912. Harry Pendock and Harry Amos are standing on trees in the carpenter's yard, behind the wall on the left. Fred Amos is in front with his bicycle.

Bridge House stands by the banks of Bradley Brook. The bridge over the river was known as Fugills Bridge. At one time this building housed licensed premises, known as the Bridge Inn. The landlord from 1851 to 1871 was Edward Bissex with his wife Maria. In the distance are Willow Bank and Hambrook Hospital.

The house later fell into an advanced state of disrepair. A feature which helps determine its age is the layer of stone tiles at the base of the roof.

Today Bridge House has been restored and allows this splendid view. What can be done with hard work and a little bit of money!

Mulgrove Farm stands on a hill outside the village on the Old Gloucester Road. Its known history dates back to 1719 when the owner was William Swayne.

On the left is Rock House, owned by Mrs Ann Rickards in 1827. It was later sold to Mr H. Ludwell of Winterbourne in 1902 as a bake-house and shop. It was here that the author's father, Jim Marks, had his first job at the age of thirteen years in 1911.

The house in the centre of this view is reputed to have been an inn in its earlier years. It became the home of Mrs Mapstone but was later taken down for the building of the M4 motorway.

Hambrook Cottages were at the end of Mill Lane and were reached by crossing a single footbridge over the River Frome.

Another view of Hambrook Cottages. Two locals are chatting by the well. As with many buildings in Hambrook, these cottages were pulled down when the M4 was built.

A meeting of the otter hounds at Luton's Meadow. Rock House is on the left. The hounds would follow the River Frome as far as Damsons Bridge. Mr Clay kept a general store at Pye Corner.

The single footbridge over the River Frome is in the centre foreground and Hambrook Cottages are on the left. On the right is Hambrook Mill and in the middle distance are the White and Black Horse inns. At the top right is Hambrook Hospital.

Three
Industry

Hambrook's main industry was the market gardening trade. There are still two working farms in the village. There have been builders, mainly the Simmonds brothers whose yard was turned into an industrial centre for small firms. At one time Kelston Caravans were made there.

Workers at Brown's Market Garden on the site in Old Gloucester Road, probably in the 1920s. From left to right: Harry Coombes Snr, Herbert Brown, Bill Brown, J.M. Taylor, Tom Clifford, Bill Anthony, Fred Criddle, -?-, Mrs Daisy Ettles, Mrs Fanny Guy, Cyril Cox, Ron Pincott, Dennis Guy, Arthur Hill, Hullet Clifford, Ern Wallace, Harry Coombes. Fred Fitz is the driver of the right-hand lorry.

Land Army girls during the war years.

Employees of Begbrook Quarry rest on the workings of their steam crane during their lunch break. The quarry was owned by Thomas Free & Sons. From left to right, back row: Charlie Adams, Bill Solace, ? Curtis. Middle row: -?-, Henry Hathaway, George Adams, -?-, -?-, Cyril Kethro, ? Harrison (crane driver).

A typical country scene at harvest time between the wars.

Hay loaded onto a horse-drawn cart.

The Wool Factory, Filton Road, Hambrook. In 1825 this building was owned by the Tucket family of Frenchay Grove and later by William Perry, who had been the factory manager. The manager's house was at the end of the building. Drying sheds can be seen on the right, which have now been made into accommodation.

At the end of its working life, the factory was converted into several houses. At the rear of the building there is a hauling door high up in the gable.

Hambrook Mill from a watercolour painted in 1906. The Mill is the oldest one on the River Frome; records of it go back to 1334.

Hambrook Mill in the 1930s. In early days, mills were owned by the Lord of the Manor, who leased them out to millers. In 1334 this mill was held by Walter Gasselyne. It has had many names in the past given by previous owners: in 1653 it was known as Jockhams Mill, in 1808 as Jakes Mill, and in 1840 Albrights. The Mill closed in the early twentieth century. One of the last millers was Mr Coombes. The mill's wheel and workings are on the right-hand side. The house later fell into disrepair and has now been rebuilt as a bungalow.

Harry Stoke Colliery was a new pit dug in 1952. It closed on 14 June 1963. The colliery was a drift mine with a gradient of 1 in 3.

Sorting coal at Harry Stoke.

A steam crane and maintenance team working on the railway in 1900.

This building once stood by The Stream in the grounds of Hambrook Grove. What was it used for? Why are the arches so high and narrow, only 6ft wide? It has now been demolished and the stone re-used in the repair of other buildings in the village.

Hambrook Garage was situated at the rear of Elleray House. It was owned by Mr and Mrs Peters. It was more than a filling station: Mr Peters was very good at reboring and rebuilding engines. Peggy Peters was a brilliant pianist and entertainer and would play at the Black Horse inn.

A view of the engineering workshop at Hambrook Garage in the 1930s.

Four
The Hospital

The hospital at Langley House, which was among the first of its kind to be established, was founded by Dr Edward Crossman and was opened on 2 January 1867. It was described as a small house (formerly two cottages) on Whiteshill, containing nine rooms. The property was on lease from Sir J.H. Greville Smyth until 1885 when it was purchased. In 1897, Dr Francis W. Crossman took over from his father who later died in 1904. It was thought that a complete rebuild of the hospital would be a good memorial to him. The new building was opened on 25 October 1905. The hospital closed in 1951 and the house is now divided into flats.

The earliest known picture of the hospital is this, taken from a watercolour by W.B. Good in 1882.

The hospital in 1905, the year in which it was re-opened (on 25 October) by Her Grace the Dowager Duchess of Beaufort.

The hospital is in the distance on the hill in this view from around the time of the First World War. The buildings on the left are Bridge House and Willow Rank, while at the extreme right is the Malthouse of the White Horse inn. Note the two men with rakes – they were probably hay-makers.

Willow Rank, seen here below the hospital, was later taken down for road improvements.

The road below the hospital was very steep and had this tight bend, causing difficulties for horse-drawn traffic. Note the sign on the right erected by a group which promoted draught horses' welfare.

In 1923 a balcony and another ward was added. Further wards were added in 1928 and 1933. The cost to a patient in 1937 was £1 17s. It was considered one of the best small hospitals (under thirty beds) in the country.

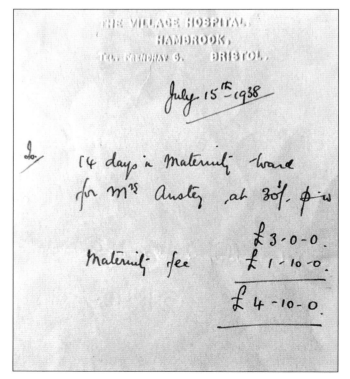

THE VILLAGE HOSPITAL,
HAMBROOK,
TEL. FRENCHAY 6.   BRISTOL.

July 15th 1938

To/   14 days in Maternity ward
for Mrs Anstey, at 30/. p.w

£ 3 - 0 - 0.

Maternity fee   £ 1 - 10 - 0.

£ 4 - 10 - 0.

A receipt from the hospital for maternity care, 15 July 1938. Mrs Anstey was landlady at the Black Horse inn and this receipt relates to the birth of her daughter, Margaret. Margaret later called her home Crossman House after the doctor who delivered her.

Five
Whiteshill House

In 1768 Whiteshill House was owned by Dr Thomas Mountjoy, who died on 22 April 1797 aged sixty-four years. The house was put up for sale with ten acres of land and was purchased by Joseph Wickwick. He gave the land on which Whiteshill Congregational church was built in 1816. Dr John Hay was a tenant for many years. Dr Edward Crossman, who had joined him as a partner, lived in nearby Whitecroft House. He took over Whiteshill House in 1856 when Dr John Hay died. Dr Crossman died in 1904 and was succeeded by his son, Dr Francis Ward Crossman JP, OBE. There were two other sons, the Rt Hon. Sir C. Stafford Crossman and Col. George Lytton Crossman DSO, CMG. Dr Edward Crossman added to the size of the house, also buying many nearby houses. It was a large house to run, employing a staff of at least twelve; these included two grooms, one of whom was the author's father, Jim Marks, and uncle, Tom Cook. Six ladies worked in the house. Dr Francis Crossman's wife, Alice, was also a doctor and carried on a private practice after her husband died.

The corner of the Common showing Whiteshill House in the centre with three forms of transport, *c*. 1920.

The sun lounge or greenhouse seen here was removed in later years.

Dr Edward Crossman, who lived at Whiteshill House from 1856 to 1904.

Dr Francis Crossman, son of Edward, in 1916.

Dr Francis Crossman was the Chief Medical Officer at Cleeve Hill House, which was a hospital for wounded soldiers in the First World War. Among this group of VAD nurses at Cleeve Hill House are the Elliott sisters of Frenchay: Nancy is on the left in the front row and Molly is third from the right on the back row.

Dr Francis Crossman at Cleeve Hill Hospital with his Bullnose Morris, registered AE6552.

May Day 1923 at Whiteshill House. Included here are Mrs Paddock, Hilda Adams, Aggie Cordy, Marjorie Cox, Maud Clack, Marjorie Bowyer, Ida Cox.

This could have been a children's party, with girls dressed up as nurses. Who is the lucky boy with all the girls?

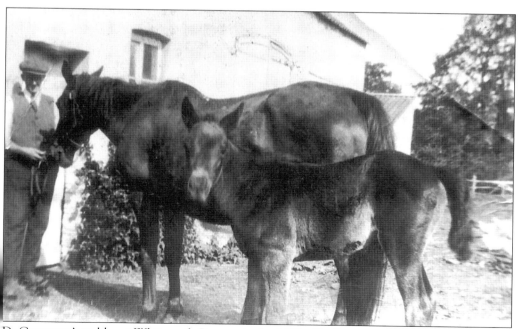

Dr Crossman's stables at Whitecroft Cottage in the 1930s. Dr Crossman's groom, Mr Jim Marks, is holding the mare. His wages were very poor in 1939 – only £2 10s per week.

Dr Crossman's horses on show at the local fête, held in the grounds of Cedar Hall, Frenchay. Mr Alf Stark leads, on the right, and is followed by Jim Marks.

Dr Alice Crossman moved to nearby Harcombes after the sale of Whiteshill House.

Six
Religion

Whiteshill Congregational church has its origins in the early nineteenth century, when cottage services were held in the hamlet of Pye Corner, five miles from Bristol. On 28 August 1816 this purpose-built church opened to serve the growing congregation.

In 1916 celebrations were organized to commemorate Whiteshill Congregational church's centenary.

Centenary tea on the lawn at Whiteshill Congregational church, 1916. Among those present are, on the middle table, Mrs Clark, Mr Jack Gifford, Mr and Mrs Lewis. Those on the right-hand table include Harold Pendock, Fowler, Harry Amos, Hilda Lewis, Pedrick Lewis, Mrs Skuse, Mrs Maggs, Rosie Maggs.

The Revd George Jarvis with his wife Mary and daughter Mary (standing). He was Minister at Whiteshill from 1912 to 1931.

The Revd G.H. Clothier was Minister from 1937 to 1945. He was a widower when he started at the church; this photograph is of his second marriage to Mrs Mann, a faithful and loyal worker at Whiteshill church.

A British day school started at the church in 1849, along with an evening class for adults. The words 'Day School' can be seen engraved over the doorway on the left. The new building on the right was added in 1991, in time for the church's 175th anniversary celebrations.

A rear view of Whiteshill Congregational church, showing the school room.

The interior of Whiteshill church, early twentieth century. Note the gas lamps hanging from the ceiling and pulpit. The choir seats in front of the organ have now been removed.

Mr & Mrs Coombes outside their cottage opposite The Crown, late nineteenth century. He was the village postman and cobbler. He also sang in the choir at Whiteshill church.

Whiteshill British School, *c.* 1894. Mrs Luff the teacher is at the left on the back row. In the centre of the front row is Amelia Player.

Whiteshill British School in 1907. From left to right, back row: Mr Luff (headmaster), Dan Manning, Joe Clevely, -?-, -?-, Elsie Bryant (teacher), -?-. Third row: -?-, Trixie Malpass, Gladys Malpass, Albert Kethro, -?-, Annie Adams, Doris Adams, Ella Kethro. Second row: Bessie Maggs, Ada Maggs, Ethel Maggs, Blanche Manning, -?-, Vera Maggs, Rose Maggs, Hilda Clevely, Fred Bracey. Front row: -?-, -?-, May Clark, -?-, Percy Thomas, Albert Fowler, Gladys Fowler.

Another early picture, showing the traditional style of the girls' dresses and the large shirt collars of the boys. The teachers are Mr Luff and Miss Pendock.

In 1910, the date of this photograph, Whiteshill British School was run by Mr Luff, assisted by his wife. Other teachers were Miss Martha Pendock, Bertha Bowen, Elsie Bryant and Miss Cohen, who lived until she was 109 and is buried at Coalpit Heath. Mr Luff played cricket and hockey. When a new school opened in 1911 most of the teachers and children transferred there.

A group of members celebrate the Ter-Jubilee (150th anniversary), 1966.

St Elizabeth's Hall, 1990s. The Hambrook Mission Room was conveyed by Mr Austen-Leigh, Rector of Winterbourne church, on 26 January 1889. It owes its origin to the Misses Ward who lived at Hambrook Grove in 1884 and rented rooms in which a Sunday school for young children was held. This led to the construction of the present building. It has recently been renovated, with mains water and a toilet being installed. It is used by local groups for social activities.

Bury Hill Mission Room, 1895. Originally built in 1867 for Church of England use, it closed 1915. In 1920/21 it was used for Nonconformist services, until the persons involved were ejected. The hall was converted into a dwelling house in the 1950s.

Bury Hill Methodist church was built using local labour in 1922, opposite the Mission Room. It closed in the 1950s. While the church was being built services were held in the open air. According to popular belief, it never rained during a service at this time!

A 1920s procession from Bury Hill Methodist church, showing the church's banner. At this time the area's name was sometimes spelt 'Berry', hence the text on the banner. From left to right: Ted Turner, Len Turner, Emma Hall, Elizabeth Cordy, Frank Mann (behind), Pearce Turner (Minister), Lionel Stallard.

A church outing to Minehead in 1925. Among the passengers are Lissie Fowler, George Noland, Emily Hall, Rose Flook, Pearce Turner, Mrs Close, Len Turner, Len Close, Bill Turner, Maggie Turner, Queenie Turney, Fred Turner, Lilly Elton, Billy Elton.

Another church outing, this time from 1927. Those present include Albert Rodman, Frank Smith, Gilbert Sandy, Mrs Ben Smith, Edna Hollister, Mrs Sandy, Dick Sandy, Norman Wiltshire, Ida Rodman, Gladys Curtis, Ivy Andrews, Ivy Skidmore, Ella Hollister, Ray Hollister, Emma Jones, Ron Drew, Eddie Maggs, George Bisp, Mrs Andrews, Mrs Lloyd, Mrs Adams, Mrs Drew.

This outing was to Gough's Cave at Cheddar in 1929. Among those present are Len Close, Herbert Bird, Len Turner, Jack Cordy, George Nolan, Emma Hall, Mrs Stanley, Lucinda Turner, Pearce Turner, Mrs Close, Mrs Turner, Doug Turner, Bill Close, Les England, Lilly Elton, Albert England, Mrs England, Bill Turner, Frank Mann.

Outing to Weston-super-Mare in 1928. From left to right: Stan Glastonbury, Hubert Flook, Bill Flook, Mrs Turner, Francis Turner, Olive Evans, Herbert Evans, Pearce Turner, Morley Turner, Hilda Close, Doris Evans, Lucinda Turner, Win Turner, Olive Turner, Mrs Close, Aggie Cordy, Rose Flook, Gladys Close, Rosie Glastonbury, Bill Close, Mrs Glastonbury, Maurice Glastonbury (baby), Phyllis Glastonbury, Maud Close.

The Winterbourne Parish war memorial on Whiteshill Common. The stone used in the monument is local pennant stone from Huckford Quarry, which was taken to Small Lane Quarry at Fishponds to be dressed. The memorial was unveiled by Miss Robinson of Frenchay on 1 January 1922. It records the names of the men who lost their lives in the war of 1914-1918 from the parishes of Frenchay, Winterbourne and Winterbourne Down. The names of those lost in the Second World War have also been added.

Seven

School

Council School, Hambrook.

Whiteshill Council School, built in 1910. The date is stamped in the drain boxes. It was opened in 1911. The wood block floor was laid by an Italian man, helped by his wife. This was a very important school in the area. It provided classes in woodwork for boys and cookery for the girls, only one session a week. On the other days pupils would visit from other schools. It had its own kitchen which provided school meals. The headmaster, Mr George Palmer, would teach many subjects including football, cricket, rounders and gardening. In the last two years the pupils had their own 'plot' for gardening. Pupils were also encouraged to take up stamp collecting. Children started school at three years and stayed until they were fifteen. At eleven some pupils went to the Grammar School at Chipping Sodbury. Later on some went to Staple Hill for special lessons. Miss Bateman was the first cookery teacher. Miss Norris was the infants' teacher, and these pupils would lie on beds in the afternoon for a sleep or rest. The school was also known as Winterbourne Council School.

Whiteshill School, 1912. From left to right, back row: Gladys Lowe, Hilda Player, Albert Goodfield, -?-, Marg Humphries, Harry Hooper, George Huish, Celia Pendock, Reg Trevelian, ? Trevelian, Ivy Huish. Third row: May Clarke, Gladys Chappell, Doris Huish, Amy Hillier, ? Luton, Charlie Hillier, Fred Bracey, Ben Huish. Second row: Arthur Bready, Bill Taylor, -?-, Marge Trevelian, Kath Humphries, Maggie Honeyball, Millicent Lowe, Ada Bird, Dolly Adams, Mabel Bird, Len Luton, Frank Huish. Front row: May Thomas, Fred Lewis, Bert Fowler, Syd Mapstone, ? Bowing, Alf Humphries, -?-, Arch Huish, Stan Sargent, -?-, ? Gifford, Gilbert Chappell.

Whiteshill School garden in 1912. From left to right, back row: Dick Johnson, Kingsley Palmer, Fred Close, Pete Maggs, Mr Luff (headmaster), Hubert Shepherson, Bill Malpass (with hat), Jack Mapstone, Percy Mulis, Charlie Hillier, Bert Fowler. Front row: Harry Edwards, Ernie Woodley, Alden Collett, Cliff Pearce, Charlie Woodley.

Whiteshill Council School in 1929. From left to right, back row: Bill Maby, Teddy Maggs, Fred Rodman, Ron Iles, Reg Stacey, Les Parker. Third row: Gwen Emery, Joyce Cleevely, Grace Teagle, Flo Taylor, Marge Thomas, Winnie Bready, Mollie Huish, Edna Stallard, Hilda Merrick, Mr George Palmer (headmaster). Second row: Olive Bird, Daisy Toogood, Betty Teagle, Sylvia Mayell, Barbara Guy, Elsie Coles, Marie Wood, Helga Woodword, Margaret Reed, Olive Fitz. Front row: Alfie Knapp, Roy Cook, Gordon Shipton, Jack Stallard, Jack Kilby, Vernon Richardson, Victor Maggs, Billy Bradley.

The school again, this time in 1930. From left to right, back row: Wilf Bryant, John Wood, Evan Gillan, Bill Carpenter, Maurice Reed, Percy Adams. Middle row: Maisie Vile, Cicely Edwards, Joan or Betty Pullin, Hilda Close, Audrey Pullin, Daisy Bready, Kath Coles, Iris Maby, Muriel Always, Kath Hurley. Front row: Gladys Adams, Hazel Maggs, Betty Woodward, Fred Hart, Frank Pullin, Don Edwards, Wilf Collett, Melvin Thomas, Doug Fitz, Les Alden.

Hambrook School running team at Chipping Sodbury Sports, 1934. They won first prize. The jerseys were black and yellow stripes. From left to right, behind: Luke Rogers, Doug Fitz. In front: Owen Fitz, Dennis Underwood, Ivor Guy. Doug Fitz and Ivor Guy both played football for Bristol City for many years.

Winterbourne Council School in 1935. From left to right, back row: Brian Rutter, Colin Manning, Tom Jackson, Derek Trowbridge, Ken Moore, Ted Blacker. Middle row: Roy Elliott, Stafford Vile, George Lawrence, Lilly Maby, Pearl Wheeler, Esme Thomas, Margaret Rodman, Beryl Vile, Billy Dumper, Eric Middle, Brian Woodbury. Front row: Zoe Maggs, Maisie Fowler, Alwyn Bartlett, Nan Hibbard, Barbara Smart, Evelyn Moulding, Doreen Green.

Winterbourne Council School, 1936. From left to right, back row: Ken Moors, Arthur Palmer, Pete Maby, Raymond Thornell, Roy Elliott, Brian Rutter, Cyril Holman, Norman Pedrick. Middle row: Albert Adams, Roy Edwards, Brenda Churchill, Zoe Maggs, Esme Thomas, Lily Maby, Margaret Rodman, Basil Withers, David Davis. Front row: Nan Hibberd, Barbara Smart, Maisie Fowler, Christine Morgan, Adelaide Jackson, May Moon.

Winterbourne Council School, 1937. From left to right, back row: Miss Evans (teacher), John Jackson, John Churchill, Raymond Thornell, Teddy Ford, Peter Moon, Raymond Bracey, -?-. Middle row: Valerie Maggs, Kathleen Adams, Sheila Edwards, June Marks, Ruby Rodman, Marie Millard, Raymond Anstey, -?-. Front row: Dolly Knapp, Heather Turner, Mary Huish, Joan Malpass, Dinah Bracey, Lily Britton, Elizabeth Hood.

Winterbourne Council School, 1936. From left to right, back row: Miss Williams (teacher), George Pullin, Lilly Britton, Mary Huish, Valerie Maggs, Lilly Millard, Sylvia Smart, Raymond Bracey, Kathleen Adams, Fred Britton, Nellie Stokes (teacher). Middle row: Peter Moon, -?-, Eunice Rogers, Ruby Rodman, Elizabeth Hood, Stella Bartlett, Eric Byatt, John Churchill, Raymond Thornell, Raymond Anstey, Teddy Ford, Clive Withers. Front row: June Bracey, Sydney Marks, Eunice Moore, John Bartlett, Margaret Maggs, Eileen Pullin, ? Maggs, Alec Badman, Heather Turner.

Hambrook School football team, 1957. From left to right, back row: Ray Phippen, Edward Harris, Gary Crew, Graham Thomas, Chris Lowe, David Sargent. Front row: Howard Thomas, Terry Brown, Paul Gosling, Roger Maggs, David Hathaway.

Eight
Hambrook Bands

Hambrook Silver Band was formed in 1897 by the Revd F.W.F. Bishop, vicar of All Saints', Winterbourne Down. Mr J. Hewitt was one of the early conductors. The first engagement was at Wick on Whit Monday 1898. The Revd Bishop left the parish in 1900. Responsibility then fell to Albert Fowler of Pye Corner. He was the conductor for many years, succeeded by Mr Jack Miles and then his son, Dick. There were a few fathers and sons in the band – George Adams and son Charlie, Jack Adams and Frank, Fred Lockyer and son Philip, brothers George and Fred Bracey. The band continued until 1974 when it moved to Thornbury and was renamed Thornbury Town Band. This is one of the first photographs of the band, taken at Cleeve Hill House, Downend (the home of Lady Cace), in around 1899. Albert Fowler is on the left of the drummer, and the third man from the right is Revd Bishop. At the far right is Jack Hewitt; Willie Evans, Jack Adams and George Adams also appear.

Hambrook Brass Band, 1918. From left to right, back row: Bert Fowler, Fred Biggs, Jim Adams, Jim Mason, Jack Miles, Albert Fowler (conductor), George Bracey, Joe Stanley, -?-, Haydon Emery (drummer), George Adams. Front row: Billy Barton, Fred Monks, Jack Adams, Fred Tilley (clown), Leonard Maggs, Worthy Blackmore. Bert Fowler and George Bracey were both eight years old when they joined the band. George went on to become secretary for fifteen years.

An unknown parade including eight Legion Standards. Those in the front row, from left, are Jack Adams, Reg Collins, Fred Lockyer, Frank Adams. Others featured include Ivan Mills, Bert Fowler, George Bracey, Gordon Moggridge (side drum), Fred Bracey (bass drum).

A Whitsun parade at Salem church, 1924. From left to right: Hayden Emery (drummer), Albert Fowler, Jack Miles, Bert Fowler, Charlie Adams, -?-, Jack Adams, -?-, Fred Monks, -?-, -?-, George Bracey, Vic Thompson, -?-, -?-, Worthy Blackmore.

A band meeting at The Cedars, Winterbourne, home of Mr and Mrs Marsh, in 1928 or 1929. From left to right, back row: George Bracey, Charlie Adams, -?-, Bert Fowler, -?-, -?-, George Marsh. Middle row: -?-, Billy Barton, Worthy Blackmore, Vic Thompson, -?-, Jack Adams.

The band at Winterbourne Collegiate School. From left to right, back row: Philip Lockier, Charlie Adams, Bert Fowler, -?-, George Adams, Bill Dixon, Arthur Drew, George Bracey, Arthur Lines, Terry Petrie. Middle row: Fred Bracey (drummer), Oliver Dutfield, Reg Collins, Harold Churchman, Ivan Mills, -?-, Vic Thompson, Arthur Tovey. Front row: Frank Adams, Jack Adams, Joe Mills (Hon. Sec.), Jack Miles (conductor), Rex Hopes (Collegiate School headmaster), Dick Miles, Fred Lockyer.

A parade at Thornbury, by the church. Dick Miles, the conductor, is leading the procession and at the back on the left is George Bracey.

Nine
Sport

The oldest sports club in Hambrook must be the Cricket Club. They started playing in 1878. The club badge is made up of emblems representing the four inns that were in the village at the time – the Black Horse, the White Horse, the Crown and the Star. This is one of the earliest photographs of the club, from around 1900. From left to right, back row: Jim Amos, Dr Frank Crossman, -?-, -?-, -?-, George Crossman. Middle row: Graham Maggs, H. Adams. Revd Ken Bishop, -?-, Frank Maggs. Front row: Jesse Maggs.

Hambrook Cricket Club, 1918. From left to right, back row: Maurice Maggs, Chris Kilby, Ken Ware. Third row: George Manning (Star Inn), Tom Player, Jack Miles, Laurie Harding, Don Harding, Jim Adams, Frank Maggs. Second row: Albert Maby, Edgar Manning, Gwylym Emery, Dan Manning. Front row: Ted Manning (scorer), Harry Woodbury, Harry Thomas, Harry Amos, Stanley Cook.

Hambrook Cricket Club, 1921. From left to right, back row: Jim Adams, Maurice Maggs, Chris Kilby, Albert Maby, Fred Fitz, Jesse Maggs, Frank Maggs. Middle row: Dan Manning, Dan Maggs, -?-, Gwilym Emery, Edgar Manning. Front row: Jack Miles, Alan Maggs, Edith Crew (later Penton), Stanley Crew, Ken Ware.

Hambrook Cricket Club in 1961. From left to right, back row: Malcolm Davis, Ralph Penton, Tony Taylor, Mike Reece, Mike Head, Les Curtis. Front row: Ken Dawbney, Tom Collett, Harry Smith, Ray Collett, Roger Northam. Sitting in front: Graham Thomas.

One of the most important parts of any cricket match is the tea break! This photograph shows teatime at a Hambrook cricket match in 1961. From front to back, left-hand side of the table: Marie Maggs, Pat Collett, Harry Smith, Master Smith, Ray Close, Mike Head, Betty England (holding baby Mandy Collett). Right-hand side: Raymond Collett, Tony Taylor, Malcolm Davis, Roger Northam, Mike Reece.

Hambrook Football Club's finest hour was winning the Gloucestershire Senior Cup at Eastville Stadium in 1949. They beat Soundwell in front of a crowd of 8,000. They are seen here being presented with the cup. From left to right: Percy Adams, -?-, Brian Woodbury, Bert Brunt, Ken Daubney, Owen Fitz, Maurice Glastonbury, Joe Clifton, Bill Manning, John Davis, Cliff Lowe, Cyril Clarke, -?- (presenting cup), Ron Drew, Reg Hooper, Archie Dixon, Vic Coles. They have also won the Berkeley Hospital Cup on several occasions, as well as the First Division of the Bristol and District League. They joined the Premier Combination, gaining promotion to the Gloucestershire County League. They are now playing in the Bristol Premier League.

Hambrook Football Club, 1930/31 season. From left to right, back row: Harry Edwards, Haden Emery, Archie Dixon, Albert Maggs, Fred Wood. Middle row: Gwilliam Emery, John Davies, Joe Adams. Front row: Ted Cook, Charlie Adams, Don Mugglesworth, Raymond Lowe, Cyril Kethro.

Hambrook Football Club. From left to right, back row: Reg Thornton, Ted Cook, Edwin Middle, Tom Brunt. Middle row: Norman Hardy, Joe Clifton, John Davis, Bert Brunt, Cyril Clarke, Brian Woodbury, Owen Fitz, Jim Rooke, Reg Hooper. Front row: Bill O'Riley, Maurice Glastonbury, Ken Dawbney, Dick Miles, Bill Manning, Mike Scadding, Ron Drew.

Hambrook Football Club in the 1947/48 season, photographed at the White Horse inn in the village. From left to right, back row: Joe Clifton, Frank Ettles, Albert Adams, Cyril Clark, Harold Thornell. Middle row: Tom Brunt, Bert Brunt, -?-, Rusty Maggs, Raymond Thornell, Brian Woodbury, Cliff Lowe, Eric Middle, Harry Cook, Desmond George, Bill Hutton (landlord), Percy Adams, Bert Clevely, Vic Coles. Front row: Harold Johns, Jimmy Rooks, Bill Manning, Ted Cook, Edwin Middle, Reg Hooper, Owen Fitz, Ken Daubney, Ron Drew. The two boys in front are Malcolm Davis and Kendle Coles.

Hambrook Football Club, 1952/53. From left to right, back row: Ray Close, Ralph Maggs, Jimmy Rooks, Percy Adams, Frank Ettles, Tom Collett, -?-, Ray Curtis, Godfrey Bisp, Ray Collett, George Cox, Chris Pullin, Harold England, Harold Johns, Ted Haskins, Frank Hackerman, Crowie May, Grenville Young, Bert Clevely, Don Pedrick. Front row: Cyril Lowe, Maurice Glastonbury, Reg Cooper, Edwin Middle, Ted Cook, Martin Rutter, George Pullin, Brian Woodbury.

The Annual Dance of Hambrook Table Tennis Club, held at the Victoria Rooms, Bristol, in 1957. From left to right: Valerie Cook, Pam Lowe, Vivienne Hacker, Ambrose Pullin, Jean Dando, Theresa Pullin, Barbara Maggs, Edna Harding, Christine May, David Pullin, Tony Edwards, John Skidmore, Malcolm Thomas, Gordon Thomas, Neil Ware.

Above left: Ivor Guy was captain of Hambrook Football Club at the age of eighteen, when they were playing in the Bristol Suburban League. He was soon spotted by a Bristol City scout and joined them as a professional player. He worked his way through the colts and reserves into the first team. He stayed with the club for fourteen years making over 600 appearances at right-back. After his death in 1986 at the age of sixty-two years, one of his team mates said 'He was a good professional. I believe he had the balance just right and football would be much richer if there were more people like Ivor in the game. He was never booked or sent off. His strong South Gloucestershire dialect used to make me think of him as a farmer coming into town for a day the market. He was such a prodigious kicker of the ball that playing against Cardiff City at Ninian Park in the 1944/45 season he scored from 70 yards.'

Above right: Doug Fitz. As a fifteen-year-old, Doug started playing football for Staple Hill Juniors at Page Park, moving a year later to Frenchay United, who were in the District League. Their home matches were played on Frenchay Common. At nineteen he signed amateur forms for Bristol City, playing full-back or centre half for the City Colts. Three years later Doug completed professional forms and played in twelve first team games. After five years at Ashton Gate he moved to Douglas, Kingswood, in the Western League. Another move took him to Glastonbury where he had five successful years, winning the Western League title and Somerset Professional Cup. Doug was also a member of Frenchay Cricket Club, starting at the age of thirteen and completing thirty-one years as an all-rounder. He was captain of the XI for a few years. In 1946 an amusing incident was reported in the *Bristol Evening Post* about a match on the Common against Stapleton. One of Doug's boundary shots sent the ball through the door of a passing bus which eventually stopped enabling the ball to be recovered. Unfortunately a broken ankle sustained while playing football ended his playing days. Since then he has followed Bristol City at Ashton Gate and his local Winterbourne side.

Above left: Gary Crewe, a Hambrook racing cyclist. Gary became a sportsman from an early age when he attended Hambrook Primary School between 1953 and 1957. He was in the school football team. He then joined Frenchay Cricket Club from 1959 to 1961 before taking up cycling. Joining the Bristol South Cycling Club, he enjoyed all the different types of cycling but his heart was in road racing, Tour de France style. In 1966 he changed clubs and joined the Western Road Club, who had a strong road team. His first big success came in 1967 when he won the Western Area Championship. In 1968 he came fifth in the British Championships. In 1970 he was first in the Isle of Man International, second in the British Championship, second in the Milk Race Hill Climbing section, fifth at the Commonwealth Games Road Race in Edinburgh and he won the Western Championship. Again in 1971 he turned professional for the Holdsworth team. He spent the year learning again as pro racing adopts different team tactics. The following year saw him win the highest honour in cycling – The Professional Championship of Great Britain. He rode several times in the Tour of Switzerland, continuing as a pro rider until 1976. He was reinstated as amateur in 1980 and took on coaching young riders. With the birth of mountain bikes he was racing again. In 1992 he was third in the British Veterans' Championship. He continues to ride his bike when time permits; he now runs a business supplying cycle parts to the trade.

Above right: Malcolm Davis was born in the Village Hospital in 1940, attended Hambrook School from 1945 to 1952, then Staple Hill Secondary Modern/Technical School from 1952 to 1957 and North Gloucester Technical College at Cheltenham until 1959. He played football for Bristol Schools in 1955/56 and joined Bristol City Football Club for the same year as an amateur, playing in the 'A' team, United and Colts, as well as a few games in the reserves. He was captain of the Youth XI in 1958/59. He turned professional in 1959 but was released in 1960. Then he followed in his father's footsteps, playing for Hambrook between 1960 and 1964 and again in 1972/73. In the summer he was playing cricket for Hambrook from 1954 to 1963. He also helped in the building of the sports pavilion. He then played for Stapleton for nine years but returned to Hambrook in 1976 and was captain and secretary for many years. He gave up football in 1991 but still plays for the cricket club. In 1978 he was captain when the Hambrook Club celebrated their centenary, playing an MCC side. He was asked if he would like to become a member. After a few qualifying games he was accepted. He is the only local person to have this honour.

Ten
Pye Corner

Pye Corner is a hamlet just off Whiteshill Common. There were only twenty-seven houses there in the 1940s and '50s. It had four shops – a butcher's, two grocer's/sweet shops and a chemist's.

In the first cottage on the left Mr and Mrs Billy Maggs lived. He was the local secretary of the 'Pioneer Sick Club'. In his spare time he was the barber and cut locals' hair in his shed. His son, Fred, was the local electrician. In the next cottage lived the district nurse, who would sell any medicines required.

Mr and Mrs Billy Maggs and their son Fred.

Pye Corner, c. 1921. The boy second from the right in the group of children appears to be Rusty Maggs. He lived in one of the nearby cottages. The motor car is a Model T Ford belonging to the local coal merchant, Mr Charlie Vile. On the left is the local shop run by Mr and Mrs Clay.

The BP and Mobil signs are advertisements for the vehicle repair business run by Mr Bill Pullin. Also, at the end of the lane, was a quarry known as Shell Hill. The quarry had a steam crane whose driver was Ted Pullin.

Mr Charles Vile loading his lorry at Winterbourne station. He also had railway coal trucks with his name on them. The business was continued by his sons Arch and Ernest for many years.

The Barton is a small cul-de-sac which ends at Bradley Brook. Years ago there was a ford across the brook, leading to Quarry Barton. The author was born in Rose Cottage in The Barton. The Barton was known as Nibletts Court before it was turned into homes.

Brookside Cottage in 1934. The author's grandmother, Mrs Alice Marks, is on the right, with Mr Bert Fowler, a notable local historian.

Brookside Cottage in the 1960s. The track to the ford can still be seen. Because the area was prone to flooding, the bed of the river was dug deeper and the ford was lost.

Brookside Cottage today. The garage on the left is built on the track to the ford.

Mr Thomas Marks proudly showing off a lettuce at Brookside Cottage.

Alice and Thomas Marks on 8 August 1935, the day they celebrated their golden wedding anniversary. Two years later both died, Thomas on 5 June and Alice seven days later.

Local children who lived in The Barton, Pye Corner, c. 1932. From left to right: Mavis Bryant, Margaret Pullin, Maisie Fowler, Maurice Taylor, Christopher Pullin. On the trike is June Marks.

Playing in the Bradley Brook. Three of the children are Mavis Bryant, Roy Cook and Len Edwards (known as Speedy).

Children love the water! These are four of the author's cousins who had come from Birmingham to visit their grandparents.

A winter's view from Pye Corner. On the right is the butcher's shop run by Mr Gilbert Ware from 1919. Before him the butchers were Fred Maggs and his father, John Maggs.

The bridge over Bradley Brook with Brookside Cottage behind. At one time the bridge was only wide enough for foot passengers. It was widened for carts and other traffic. If one cares to walk under the bridge the joins can be seen. On a map of 1889 it is marked as a footbridge. It could have been widened at the time the railway was built between 1897 and 1903.

Pye Corner in foreground, with Quarry Barton in the distance. The cottage in the middle is the author's birthplace. On the right are the outbuildings of April Cottage.

The outbuildings of April Cottage with Worthy Marks and the author's sister, June Marks, in 1932.

The Cook family lived in a wooden bungalow, an ex-Army hut from the First World War. They are seen here in the late 1920s. From left to right: Rapkin, Alice, Bertha and Laura. In later years Austin Luton lived there.

This cottage in Quarry Barton is reputed to have been once the Plume of Feathers inn. At the time of this photograph it was the Harris' family home. In one of the outhouses are large ovens, so it could also have been a bakery.

Tom Walker, a well-known character around the village, was born in 1893. When he was twenty-one years old he joined the Salvation Army. He was called up to join the Army in the First World War but refused to fight in the front line on religious grounds. He was shunned by some people for refusing to kill others. He served as a stretcher-bearer and a hairdresser in Egypt. After the war he became a local postman. One day at Northwoods he was attacked and badly beaten up. This may have been the turning point in his life, when he took to the road. Every Wednesday he would visit his niece, Grace Harris, at Quarry Barton. He would stay for lunch; his favourite meal was smoked haddock. He always had a wild flower in his button hole and cap and his bicycle was decorated with coloured wool and ribbons. Always a friendly man, he had many friends in the surrounding villages who would give him a meal. He never had to ask. He kept up his religious beliefs and the local children would ask him for the text of the day. He would quote them a verse from the Bible. He slept in a shed on a local farm. Tom died on 31 January 1961 aged sixty-eight years. He is buried in Winterbourne churchyard.

Sturden Court Cottages. It appears that this building was the original Courthouse. It is possible that it dates back to 1286. Before 1776 it belonged to Harford Lloyd who conveyed it to Robert Tucker of Winterburne. In 1869 it was converted into four cottages. In the 1940s the tenants were Kethros, Bracey, Hollyman and Taylor.

Mrs Bracey with her son, John, in 1937. Mrs Bracey died aged ninety-five in 2001.

Sturden Court Farm in the 1980s. The farm was originally held by the Smyth family, Lords of the Manor of Sturden. It is connected by tradition with the elopement of Hugo De Stern who was in love with a lady living at Syston. Her father gave chase and in attempting to kill Hugo, slew instead his own daughter. A room in the house is supposed to be haunted by her, in the form of the 'White Lady'. It is believed the glee 'O who will o'er the Downs so free' (see page 2) was written in the dining room at Sturden Court Farm.

The cowshed at Sturden Court Farm. Farming ceased here many years ago. When the author worked here as a boy for 6d an hour, Jack Withers was the farmer. His right-hand man and 'Jack of all jobs' was Joe Woolley. The farm and barns are now being converted into accommodation units.

The Star inn at Pye Corner. From 1897 until 1953 it was run by the Manning family; then the Pinnells took over for the next thirty-five years. The inn closed in 1989.

Outside the Star, c. 1915. From left to right: Gladys Morgan (the landlady's niece), Edgar Manning (the landlady's son), Cicely Smart, Alan Peters, sisters Agnes and Ethel Smart, Fred Amos.

Hambrook Football Club, at the Star in the 1913/14 season. The inn was used as a changing room.

The Star Music Men, *c.* 1910. From left to right: Albert Fowler, J. Horsman, J. Whitby, George Adams. ? Taylor, Dogger Adams.

Guides and Brownies from Winterbourne Down congregate for May Day 1986 at the Star.

Winterbourne Down Ladies' Boarder Morris Team. In the centre foreground is Mrs Pat Davis.

Three local characters dressed up for May Day! They are Terry Martin, Audrey Marks and Alan Mildren.

Star Cottage, adjoining the Star inn, is where the Marks family lived from 1937 to 1949. There was no electricity – only oil lamps – and the water tap was outside along with the toilet, a soakaway, that had to be cleaned out every few years. The rent was 4s 6d per week.

Opposite the Star and down a flight of steps was this cottage, the home of the Adams family. On the right is Mr Adams and to the left are Mrs Lizzie Adams, Mary Ann, Minnie (later Fowler) and Lottie (later Manning), landlady of the Star inn. During the war the Mahoney family lived here. Mr Mahoney used to play his accordion to the cinema queues in Bristol. His nickname was the 'Travelling Minstrel'.

Minnie Adams and Albert Fowler on their wedding day, 26 December 1899. They were married at Winterbourne Down church.

Minnie Adams' mother dressed up for her daughter's wedding.

Albert and Minnie Fowler with their family in 1915. From left to right, back row: Ivy, Gladys, Phyllis (Phyllis and Ivy were twins). Middle row: Albert, Minnie. Front row: Queenie, Bert, Ethel, Albert.

Mr Albert Fowler, seen here in the 1930s, was a well-known stonemason. His work can be seen in local churchyards. He would rent a quarry and employ people to help; one such place was the Snake Quarry at Quarry Barton. It is interesting to note that his father-in-law, Frederick Adams, ran the same quarry in 1870.

Next door to the Fowlers' house was this bungalow, where Mrs Margaret Maggs lived.

Sturdens Lea, home of the Manning family, who were related to the owners of the Star. This view clearly shows where the house has been extended, where the colour and size of the stones changes. In the older side, on the right, the builder has left his trademark, a face carved on a stone, pictured left.

Woodbine Cottage. William Player bought this cottage at a public auction on 14 January 1884 for £29. The previous owner was Sir John Henry Greville Smyth, who owned a lot of land in the village. Mr Player is seen with his family outside the cottage.

Ada Maggs with her niece, Linda Woodbury (now Glastonbury). Sturden East Cottage is in the background.

Linda and Brian Woodbury and their dog Nipper pose on a 1920 Douglas 350cc motorbike, c. 1927.

Edward and Emma Maggs with their ten children. From left to right, back row: Vera, Sid, Bessie, Graham, Ada, Maurice, Blanche. Front row: Edgar, Billy, Edward, Emma, Agnes.

Laurel Cottage in the early twentieth century, when it was the home of the Luton family. In 1930 the Guys lived there. On the first and third Tuesdays of each month the local Registrar of Births and Deaths would hold office in the cottage.

Laurel Cottage today looks much the same. Only the windows having been replaced. The house on the right replaced two old cottages; it blends in well.

The three ladies on the left, Minnie Clifford, Ethel Guy, Daisy Byles, are sisters who all lived into their nineties. With them, on the right, is Joan Guy.

On the left is the shop on the edge of Whiteshill Common, run by Mr and Mrs Chris Kilby. They lived in Rose Cottage opposite. The young man is Ivor Guy.

Eleven

Moorend

Moorend is an area to the east of Whiteshill Common, which follows the River Frome round to Winterbourne Down. There are only fourteen houses.

An early photograph of Griffen Farm, taken about 1895. It was owned by the Griffiths family in the eighteenth century.

Griffen Farm today. It has been modernized, with bay windows added, and is no longer a farm. In the 1940s the Millard family lived there.

Marigold Court, home of the Tucker family for over 300 years. They were associated with Mangotsfield church. There is a brass plate on the north wall of the church inscribed 'Jno. Tucker 1657 aged 59 years. Obadiah Tucker 1680 aged 80 years. Jonathan Tucker 1712 aged 75 years. All of Moorend'. Jonathan Tucker was the donor of the peal of bells and clock to Mangotsfield church in 1687. The house is a good example of sixteenth-century domestic architecture. One fireplace reaches from floor to ceiling. On the mantlepiece are the initials 'JT 1675'.

Moorend House in 1895. The exact age of the house is not known, but the blocked-up windows give a clue. Window tax levied a sum per window in each property and was imposed in 1695. Owners used to circumvent the tax by blocking up some of their windows. In 1857 Mr Pegler had a private school here. It was put up for sale in 1885 and the sales details were: '22 rooms, 8 bedrooms, 3 acres of land, a croquet lawn, a vinery 80ft x 15ft with 15 vines'. In 1890 it was owned by S. Robertson and it housed tea rooms in 1907. From 1918 Mr and Mrs Bond lived there until 1953 when the current owner, the Chestermans, took over.

The Smithy at Moorend in 1895. The smith from 1890 until the closure of the smithy in the 1920s was Jim Packer.

Moorend Smithy in 1920.

The bricked-up remains of the wheel-pit outside the smithy in 1985. The pit was used to 'sweat' new rims onto wheels. The smithy building has now been converted into a dwelling called Rose Cottage.

For a time after the closure of the smithy, the building housed a shop and café run by Mr James Burgess, as seen here in 1925. From left to right, back row: Herbert Badman, Ted Manning, James Burgess, Harry Edwards, Les Burgess. Front row: Arch Huish, Gilbert Chappel, Charlie Adams.

Four lads in their Sunday best outside James Burgess's café, which was a well-known place for a game of cards. From left to right: Gilbert Chappel, Charlie Adams, Ted Manning, Arch Huish.

Moorend Mill in Edwardian times. The mill was tiny, so that the undershot waterwheel came up to the eaves of the single-storey building beside it, no more than a stone-built hut. Its only use was a file mill; it is probable that the mill only ground the blank bars of iron into shape. The bars may have come from the Frenchay Iron Company, further downstream, and were probably 'cut' after grinding at the nearby smithy. The mill was on an island in the middle of the stream and was probably in operation from some time in the eighteenth century to the last quarter of the nineteenth, which is when the Frenchay Iron Company was at work. The smithy associated with it was between the road and the river on the left bank and was pulled down around 1972. The weir has a fall of water of about 5ft; the wheel looks about 7ft 6ins high and 4ft wide with flat floats completely unenclosed and immersed not more than a foot or so deep. The mill itself is hardly visible behind both wheel and vegetation. There is nothing left of the mill now but the weir footings can just be discerned and the grindstones have been used as foundations for walls built in the river and as decorative features on garden walls and gateposts.

Near Moorend Mill was a track which allowed cows access to the river.

Moorend Mill in ruins.

The Riverside Walk at Moorend was a country walk popular with daytrippers from Bristol.

The Elms once belonged to Moorend Farm and the Rutter family. It contained a malt house and brewery in 1890 run by Mr Alf Tuckett.

Moorend Farm. In 1651 it became the home of Richard and Elizabeth Bayly who purchased it from William Langey of Rodway Manor. The original house stood on the opposite side of the road. Richard Bayly took down a portion of it, using the materials to build the present house. In the gable over the porch is a stone inscribed REB 1676, marking the date when the house was rebuilt. On a stone in the stables are the same initials and the date 1701. Also in the stables Cromwell's Arms are inscribed. He and his soldiers are believed to have stayed here before he went on to Bristol. In 1765 a complaint was entered against Thomas Bayly of Moorend that he 'did make pits and carry away soil and turf at Bury Hill and did become a nuisance to his neighbours.' The house stayed in the Bayly family until 1790 when it was purchased by Thomas Rutter who came from Cheshire. Mr John Rutter came in 1916. He died in 1987 aged ninety-six years. His wife, Doris, lived until 1997, aged ninety-five years. The farm was run by their son, Martin, until 1999 when he retired and sold up.

An early view of one of the old buildings opposite Moorend Farm. This could be the building where Mr Joseph Till lived. Behind this house were three cottages known as Tills Barton. In the 1920s the tenants were the Wheeleers at No. 1, Mabel Bracey, mother of George and Fred, at No. 2 and Thurza Maggs at No. 3.

The barn at Moorend Farm.

Among the various tenants of Moorend Farm was Richard Champion, who was one of the earliest manufacturers of porcelain.

A close-up of the children on previous picture. They could be from Tills Barton.

Moorend Farm with the Rutter family on the lawn in 1930.

A close up of the Rutter family from the previous photograph. From left to right: Doris, Bevan, Martin, Eileen, Judy the dog, June and Brian.

Bury Hill Camp is an Iron Age fortification. Remains dating from the third and fourth centuries BC have been found here. The fort covers about seven and a half acres. The ramparts of earth are preserved on three sides; the fourth side has been lost to quarrying.

The Red Pool. This quarry is the cause of the erosion to Bury Hill Camp. The quarry had to close when it flooded, creating this pool. In the 1940s and '50s it became the local swimming pool. Young lads would dive or jump the 100ft from the top; others would climb halfway and dive from the ledge as one lad had just done. They would come from Downend and Fishponds to swim here.

A small cottage in the woods at Moorend. Mrs Coles who once lived here is said to have brought up ten children in this small place.

A painting by W.V. Tippett of a footbridge across the River Frome with Waterfall Farm in the distance, 1897.

Waterfall Farm house. In 1827 this property was owned by George Worrall. It appears that Worrells Lane was named after him, but it is now spelt with an 'E' rather than an 'A'. In 1890 Mr Featherstone passed it on to H. Ward. It was then bought by Christopher Churchill, a market gardener. It passed in turn to his son, Sidney, grandson John, who died aged sixty-eight on 10 January 2000, and now his great-grandson James.